Santa Fe Railway's
Streamlined Observation Cars

February 1938 shot (taken in Chicago) of the two Budd coach-observation- equipped *EL CAPITAN's* flanking the Pullman-Standard sleeper-observations of the *SUPER CHIEF* and *CHIEF*. (BNSF Archives.)

By Jonathan J. Boyle, Sr.

2004
TLC Publishing, Inc.
18292 Forest Rd.
Forest, VA 24551

Dedication

This book is dedicated to and in loving memory of

Russell William Boyle

1912-2002

During his career with the Santa Fe Railway, from 1937 until his retirement in 1974, my Great Uncle exemplified the very highest standards of integrity and service as did the trains he worked and we rode together. Without his influence, this book would not have been written, nor could it have been. Like the Santa Fe trains he served, "his kind shall not pass this way, again", in both cases to my profound regret.

Mr. Boyle is shown in the photo at left, as he prepared to board the last regularly scheduled Santa Fe passenger train, #24, the former *GRAND CANYON* at Fort Madison, Iowa, on Sunday, May 2, 1971. On its arrival in Chicago four hours and 23 minutes later at 9 P.M., the books were officially closed on Santa Fe's passenger operations and the doors were locked at Dearborn Station, both for the final time. Two days earlier, he also had the privilege of being Conductor on the last train #17, the *SUPER CHIEF/EL CAPITAN*, the last westbound Santa Fe passenger train and indeed the last train to depart Dearborn Station.

At right, he is shown in the vestibule of one of *EL CAPITAN's* high-level chair cars, speeding through the Illinois darkness on #17.

Introduction and Acknowledgemets

For as long as I can remember I have been enamored of passenger trains, must admit to being overwhelmingly prejudiced in favor of the Santa Fe Railway, and their masterful operation of them, and have to say that I have never changed my opinion. As mentioned in the dedication of this book, my late Great Uncle, R.W. Boyle, was a Conductor on the A.T&S.F.; and in my connection to things railroad, his influence was irreplaceable. Up until his death in October, 2002, we had long detailed discussions on a regular basis about trains that passed from the scene from a span over sixty-five years ago until his retirement in 1974. Even at age 90 his memory was phenomenal.

In the 1960's, I corresponded with the late Stan Repp, railroad illustrator and well-known chronicler of the *SUPER CHIEF*. In the book *Santa Fe: Steel Rails through California*, by Donald Duke and Stan Kistler, he opined that "not enough attention was paid to the observation end of trains," and I couldn't agree more. A number of photos from Mr. Repp's collection appear in this volume, along with a great many other tremendous selections from other photographers and collections, the vast majority of which have not been previously published, all of which I feel most fortunate to have been granted the privilege to reproduce and include here.

While I am anxious to thank and recognize all those who have encouraged me in the venture of authoring this book, I, too, am concerned that no one deserving of at no one deserving of recognition be left out: First, and most importantly my family....I wish dedications were typically made to more than one person at a time; for they are all most certainly deserving of it: to my wife, Carolyn, for her encouragement and understanding, our children, Jonathan, Jr., Patrick, Joseph, (all of whom have been particularly helpful in the computer realm) and Bridget, along with my parents, Dr. Fred and Charla Ann Boyle who have all been most supportive of this project, in spite of it's occasional frustrations, along with all it's many enjoyments. They all, as well as my late sister, Pam, have over the years been most patient with my passenger train travel and collecting; both photos and memorabilia. For this I thank them all. For those that have been willing to contribute photographic material or give their permission for its use, in addition to my own collection; I want to give a special word of thanks: Arizona Railway Museum, "Bart" Barton, Gordon Bassett, Richmond S. Bates, Dr. Alan Bradley, Al Chione, Gary Dolzall, John Dziobko, Tom Gildersleeve, Gordon Glattenberg, Mike Gruber, Robert Haben, Dr. Robert Harmen, Ed Janosky, Kansas State Historical Society, M.D.

McCarter, Don Olsen, William Raia, the late Stan Repp, Robert Schmidt, Lloyd Stagner, Harry Stegmaier, Chard Walker, and Jay Williams.

Dr. Alan Bradley, along with the contributions from his extensive slide collection, has also assisted in editing the text as well as making a number of helpful suggestions as the work progressed. In addition to their photographic images, Gordon Glattenberg and Robert Schmidt were co-operative in making sure those were transmitted properly. Robert Haben contributed generously from his collection of vintage Santa Fe advertising. From the time I journeyed to research the photographic files housed at the Kansas State Historical Society, I wish to thank Stephen Priest who helped me get started in my search there, as well as the helpful staff members at that location. All those that have contributed to the final product in all the ways described and many others certainly again have my gratitude. In addition, telephone conversations with Wallace Abbey and Lloyd Stagner have also been most helpful.

Appreciated also, is the opportunity afforded by Thomas Dixon of TLC Publishing to document the service of streamlined observation cars of the magnificent Santa Fe Railway and to Ken Miller for his work and assistance with this venture.

Jonathan J. Boyle, Sr.
5 March 2004

The author, Jonathan J. Boyle, Sr. has been a passenger train enthusiast, especially of the Santa Fe, his entire life. Starting at an early age, he was granted the distinct privilege of making a number of trips with his Great Uncle, R.W. Boyle, a Santa Fe Railway Conductor, on his run from Fort Madison, Iowa to Chicago and return. Riding such trains as the *SUPER CHIEF, EL CAPITAN, KANSAS CITY CHIEF, TEXAS CHIEF*, and the *GRAND CANYON*, he had the rare opportunity, experienced by few, to not only ride the trains, but to absorb innumerable facts about them from the best of teachers. A licensed mortician, he and his wife Carolyn are the parents of four children and have a new granddaughter. Previously, he wrote "Rock's One of a Kind La Mirada" in February 1996 *Passenger Train Journal*.

Table of Contents

2004
TLC Publishing, Inc.

International Standard Book Number: 1-883089-98-0
Library of Congress Catalog Card Number :
Design, Layout, Type and Image Assembly by
Megan Johnson
Print On Demand, Co.
Forest, Virginia

Produced on the Mac OS™
Printed by Walsworth Publishing Company
Marceline, Missouri 64658

Super Chief

Round-end signature cars of the Santa Fe comprised a roster of twenty-five. Produced by three manufacturers: Edward G. Budd, (nine cars) Pullman-Standard, (fifteen cars) and American Car and Foundry, (one car) they were delivered from 1937 to 1950, providing three accommodation types: sleeper-observation (thirteen cars), parlor-observation (two cars) and coach-observation (ten cars).

The sleeper-observation lounges were constructed for the two premier all- Pullman streamliners that were the cornerstone of luxury travel the Santa Fe had to offer: the *SUPER CHIEF* and the *CHIEF*. Over the years, the cars served both flagship trains.

The SUPER CHIEF

Inaugurated in May, 1936, the heavyweight *SUPER CHIEF* started life sporting "Crystal View," a car from the *CHIEF* pool. It featured two drawing rooms, three compartments, and a lounge, with a brass-railed open platform.

When the first lightweight *SUPER CHIEF* made its westbound debut a year later, the crown jewel in its consist was "Navajo," its unique observation lounge. Constructed solely of stainless steel, (as was the entire Budd-built consist), it was singular in a number of respects: the only sleeper-observation to be produced for the A.T.&S.F. by that car builder, (although Pullman-operated), the only one in the fleet to have its sleeping accommodation configuration, and one of only two Santa Fe lightweight observation cars that survive to this day with their original round-ends.

Its interior was certainly designed to remain in the memory of the traveling public long after their trip on it was over. So far did it depart from the "norm" of its day that it bears specific description here (as does its

A year prior to the maiden run of the first lightweight *SUPER CHIEF*, its heavyweight ancestor is shown backed into Chicago's Dearborn Station prior to its inaugural run west. Personalities of the day such as entertainers Eddie Cantor and his family, dancer Eleanor Powell, and motion picture actor Edward G. Robinson were among the passengers aboard on that first trip. Look straight ahead for a glimpse into brightly-lit "Crystal View," its open platform overwhelmingly bedecked with blossoms for the historic run. The gentleman standing directly beneath the drumhead was Samuel T. Bledsoe, then President of the Santa Fe. (The Kansas State Historical Society, Topeka, Kansas.

arms. Intentional flaws were included in its weaving to make it appear more "authentic." Originally the lounge seated thirteen, with an additional chair placed at the writing desk. Following refurbishment in 1946, an additional lounge chair was added. "Navajo," its heavyweight predecessor, and lightweight successor used the drumhead first designed for the *SUPER CHIEF*....railroad insignia, train name, and an Indian chief's head in red and yellow set against a background of purple. Consistent with all Budd-built round-ends of the Santa Fe, placement of the tailsign made it flush with the car's exterior, which had no rear door. The last revenue service heard of was on a troop train, on which my Great Uncle, R.W. Boyle, was Conductor. He recalled passengers pulling the lounge chairs out from the walls to shoot craps. After 1950, it was a seldom-used "relief" car that protected observation car service on both the *CHIEF* and *SUPER CHIEF*. Following its retirement in 1957, it languished in storage until April 1, 1966 when it was donated to the Intermountain Chapter of the National Railway Historical Society. Today it can be seen at the Colorado Railroad Museum in Golden, where it was placed in 1971. This author and my eldest son were privileged to photograph its interior in 1985. The brightly hued upholstery fabric and ceremonial lamp with goatskin shade were long-gone. The "arrow"-shaped lights placed between the second and third windows on either side of the solarium had long since had their red tips replaced with gold-painted ones, but "Navajo" had and retains its class.

immediate successor, later): passengers were offered one bedroom, three compartments, and two drawing rooms. As with the other sleepers of the train, frequent use was made of a number of various hardwood veneers, such as satinwood that covered one of "Navajo's" drawing room walls. Curiously, with the exception of the writing desk, its chair and magazine racks, woodwork was largely absent from the lounge portion of the car, which was perhaps its most outstanding feature: copper-coloured walls, with Indian sand paintings mounted on cork between the windows, topped by a turquoise ceiling. Imitation "Indian blanket" upholstery showed a white and blue pattern on red chairs, with indigo

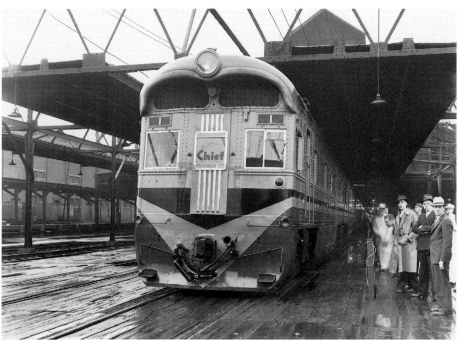

At the opposite end of the first (heavyweight) *SUPER CHIEF* were the two boxcabs, 1 and 1A, known as "Amos and Andy". Shown here at Dearborn Station in May, 1936, just prior to departing on the premier run of train #17. (The Kansas State Historical Society, Topeka, Kansas.)

Formerly part of the "Amos and Andy" duo that piloted the first (heavyweight) *SUPER CHIEF*, #1 is shown here in Argentine, Kansas, February 2, 1948. The Santa Fe made a valiant attempt to integrate the pioneer units into the growing "warbonnet" fleet; the result being an ill-tempered-looking unit that headed up the *CHICAGOAN* and *KANSAS CITYAN* on a regular basis. 1953 would see the unit rebuilt, re-emerging as 83A. (Arthur B. Johnson, author's collection.)

When the *SUPER CHIEF* initiated twice-weekly service in 1938, "Puye" its second lightweight sleeper-observation car (super-structure constructed of carbon steel, stainless steel-clad) was to have carried the markers. Significantly, neither it nor the entire second *SUPER CHIEF* consist were yet available. Instead, an entire *CHIEF* trainset was pressed into service using round-end "Chaistla" for nearly five months until all was in readiness for the mixed Pullman-Standard and Budd train to begin service.

Externally, the fundamental difference in shaping of the round-end between the two builders was immediately and markedly obvious. Budd, at the time on its non-articulated observation cars, (with the notable exception of the 1936 *DENVER ZEPHYR*) used a design that was blunt, non-tapered, and in the strictest sense round (sometimes referred to as "boat-tailed") rather than the sleek, tapered ("swallow-tailed" or "tear-drop") shape that Pullman-Standard employed extensively. (Exceptions include the coach observations of *EL CAPITAN* and the parlor observations of C&NW *TWIN CITIES 400*.)

"Puye", in some ways singular in the annals of Pullman car construction mimicked "Navajo" in a few ways: its hind-end contained no door and its tailsign was somewhat depressed into its exterior (even though all other Santa Fe sleeper-observation cars from the same builder featured the rear door, with the drumhead merely fastened on, and plugged into a conveniently-placed exterior outlet), where it was wired directly and out-of-

sight. The Indian-patterned upholstery was again used, if only in part.

Interior sleeper space in "Puye" consisted of one double bedroom and four drawing rooms, in addition to the observation lounge (a plan which would be followed in the remainder of similar cars still to be produced for the railroad in future years, and never duplicated for another.) Total seating in the lounge provided for seventeen. Additional updates made since the first car's construction included improved lighting in the lounge with the addition of table lamps and continuous lighting encircling the room's ceiling rather than ceiling-centered fixtures, (although "Navajo" did feature slatted downward-focused lighting from the curved portion of the car forward above the windows), a porthole-equipped door was added which led to the corridor leading to the front of the car and four deep-blue armchairs in the solarium of the car joined their brightly-hued companions facing inward along the sidewalls. Venetian blinds were provided with no draperies, which was just vice versa in "Navajo," which had window shades.

The two cars served the *SUPER CHIEF* during the war years until trains #17-18 began providing daily service in 1948. Pullman-Standard again provided the cars needed: "Vista Canyon," "Vista Cavern," "Vista Heights," and "Vista Valley." These cars, while possessing a conservative and perhaps understated elegance were typical examples of the then-current Pullman-Standard interior design and lacked the individuality and uniqueness of their two lightweight ancestors. They did, however, contain extra tall sets of Venetian blinds, that, in conjunction with the draperies, gave the illusion that the windows in the lounge were much taller than they actually were. Moving forward in the car's lounge, bench seating was placed on either side next to a slim triangular-shaped table that provided a distinctive "moderne" appearance. Lounge seating and desk chair provided lounge accommodation for seventeen. As in all such cars designed for the *SUPER CHIEF*, a large photo-mural, book-case-styled magazine rack, and writing desk decorated the forward bulkhead.

Another car- "Vista Club"-was constructed in 1950

by American Car and Foundry using the Pullman-Standard plans. It did not project the lusher interior character of its sister cars, appearing more utilitarian, featuring different ceiling lighting and style of lounge chair. Lacking also were the extra tall blinds and draperies. It was easily differentiated from its Pullman-Standard sisters by the square-rather-than-oblong window placed low in its rear door as well as slightly different stainless steel fluting. However, it did complete the sequence of cars of this type needed to protect ordinary service and was no doubt largely responsible for "Navajo's" later years obscurity, especially in light of the consistent sleeping accommodation space it provided. Following remodeling in 1947, one of the *CHIEF* pool of

observation cars, "Coconino," was renamed "Vista Plains" and was permanently assigned to *SUPER CHIEF* service. By the time this new series of cars was instituted, the drumhead design had changed to a yellow background, sporting an Indian chief's profile and Santa Fe logo, a pattern that would prevail until the use of tailsigns was discontinued in 1968.

Round-end observation car use on trains #17-18 continued until 1956, when they were singly returned to Pullman-Standard to be re-built to full width and made compatible to mid-train use. Unfortunately, the era of transcontinental use of these beautiful vehicles was almost at an end on the Santa Fe, as well as a number of other railroads. Common excuses for this included their "inflexibility" in consists as well as additional switching costs incurred in servicing that made them financially unpopular with the management. Typically, A.T.&S.F. made sure that the remodeling was done in a way that still provided a tasteful and attractive appearance to the car, especially when used as originally intended....on the rear of a train. During rebuilding, the round end was completely removed, a square end fashioned and added, and with original fluting from the car itself added to bracket each side of the newly-added diaphragm, above which was placed a two-lensed side-by-side red and clear-bulbed light. (The fluting did not wrap around the corner of the car's end.) Rear-facing windows were retained and the cars fortunately graced the back of the *SUPER CHIEF* until it was permanently consolidated with *EL CAPITAN* in 1958. (Reconstruction of the cars didn't alter their passenger-carrying abilities in any way.) They were then placed in service on the *SAN FRANCISCO CHIEF* as mid-train Pullman lounges (placed directly behind the diner) serving first class patrons, until their retirement and removal from service in the Summer of 1968. Regrettably, "Puye," "Vista

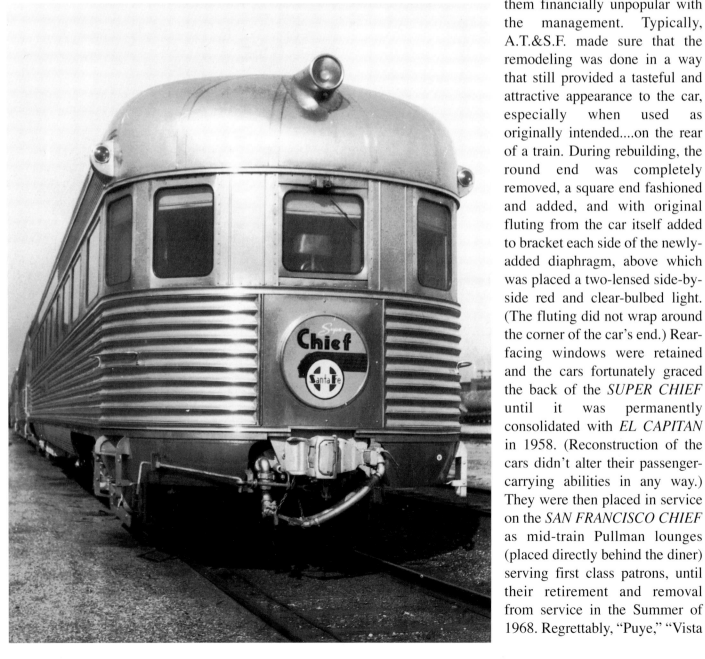

In a regal pose, Budd-built, Santa Fe-owned, Pullman operated, "Navajo" is shown here proudly punctuating the brand-new consist of the first streamlined *SUPER CHIEF* in 1937. (William A. Raia collection.)

Heights," and "Vista Club" were scrapped. The latter initially passed into private hands and was later sold to Amtrak in 1974 and dismantled the following year, (possibly providing parts for its aging "Heritage" fleet), never having been placed in its last owner's service. "Vista Canyon" now is a part of the Arizona Railway Museum collection in Chandler, following private ownership, and occasionally is still used in special service. "Vista Cavern" is in dinner train service and "Vista Valley" was recently re-sold.

The striking interior of "Navajo" is on display, as two young ladies, Eleanor Fisher and Arlette Abell look out the side window at the solarium end of the car. Note the scarlet-plumed "arrow" lamps near the amll doors in the upper portion of the side walls, giving inside access to the marker lights. (The Kansas State Historical Society, Topeka, Kansas.)

Forward bulkhead of "Navajo" was the first to display the mural depicting life among members of it's namesake tribe. By the time my eldest son and I toured the car in 1985 a mural remained, but the scene had been changed. (BNSF Archives.)

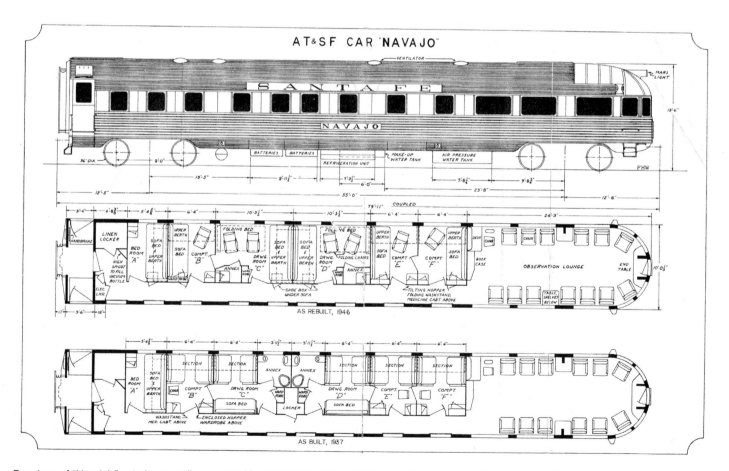

Drawings of "Navajo's" exterior as well as comparitive renderings of the interior as-built and as-re-built, nine years afterward. (Intermountain Chapter, National Railway Historical Society - Author's collection)

THE "NAVAJO"

The Navajo poses with the other cars of the new Super Chief just prior to going into service on a 39 3/4 hour schedule between Chicago and Los-Angeles on May 18, 1937. Today, as then, the Super Chief is among the finest Trains in America. Below the Super Chief is shown powered by diesel No. 3.

left - Santa Fe photo
below - Otto Perry

SPECIFICATIONS - NAVAJO

Builder .... Budd Co.
In Service ..... May, 1937
Length ...... 79 ft. 11 in.
Weight loaded 103,900 lbs.
Journal Size ... 5½ x 10 in.
Bearing Type ...... Roller
Air conditioning ......
                steam ejector
Heating .... Vapor
Electric Power ... 32 v d.c.
Capacity - sleeping   14
         - observation   14

Donated by the Santa Fe Ry. to the Intermountain Chapter, National Railway Historical Society ..... April 1, 1966

left - Looking toward the rear of the observation lounge. Budd Co. photo, H. C. Wroton collection.

The National Railway Historical Society was founded in 1935 and today has over fifty local chapters in the United States and Canada. The Intermountain Chapter was formed in 1961 and has actively pursued the Society's goals of preserving railroading's past while taking an active role in railroading as modern transportation. The Society has published several books and maps on railroad history and maintains several pieces of rolling stock used on Chapter excursions. Those interested in the society are invited to inquire to:

THE INTERMOUNTAIN CHAPTER, NATIONAL RAILWAY HISTORICAL SOCIETY
P. O. BOX 5181, TERMINAL ANNEX, DENVER, COLORADO, 80217

(The Intermountain Chapter, National Railway Historical Society; author's collection.)

Left: This portrait in profile shows the shallow rim that frames the flush drumhead installation of "Navajo". the interior of the car has now been removed due to leakage from roof damage, but it is hoped that full restoration will soon be made. (Robert Haben photo.)

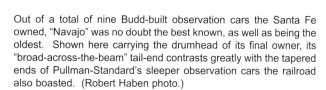

Out of a total of nine Budd-built observation cars the Santa Fe owned, "Navajo" was no doubt the best known, as well as being the oldest. Shown here carrying the drumhead of its final owner, its "broad-across-the-beam" tail-end contrasts greatly with the tapered ends of Pullman-Standard's sleeper observation cars the railroad also boasted. (Robert Haben photo.)

Floor plan of the only sleeper observation ever built by Budd for the Santa Fe, and the only one on the line that had its interior accommodations..."Navajo."

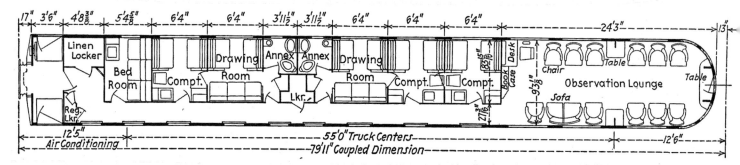

Lost in the mists of time is the reason for the Public Relations Department posing a panda in "Puye". The only sure thing here is this cars identity. Among all the one double bedroom, four drawing room sleeper observations of the Santa Fe, "Puye" was the only one that didn't include a read door (or a drumhead trailing a cord plugged directly into the car's curved end,) making one wonder out of two series totaling twelve cars, why this one varied in this structural detail? Note the abundance of grab irons on the left side, along with the drumhead first designed for the SUPER CHIEF. (The Kansas Sate Historical Society, Topeka, Kansas.)

"Puye's" observation solarium shared a few of "Navajo's" characteristics shown here are the multi-colored furniture covering and the sand paintings between the windows. Different though, were the steel-shaded table lamps, (first used in the 1938 CHIEF cars, that measurably heightened the lighting in the lounge,) ceiling lighting, as well as the lack of draperies. (Pullman-Standard.)

The head-end of "Puye's" lounge with its port-holed door, leading forward to the corridor. (These were also initially featured in the 1938 CHIEF observation cars.) "Puye" also made use of hardwood veneering in the furnishings. (Pullman-Standard.)

The "Vista" cars were constructed about the same time as the tall-windowed raised "Lookout Lounges" of Rock Island's "La Mirada", New York Central's "Sandy Creek" and "Hickory Creek", and the "Royal"-series cars of the Louisville and Nashville, Southern, and New York Central Railroads. Although the floor level was not raised in the Santa Fe cars, this interior view at first glance gave the impression that they, too, possessed the tall windows. Unfortunately, it was only an illusion, as illustrated by the outside light filtering through the Venetian blinds. (Pullman-Standard.)

The photographer captioned this photo: "Northbound at Joliet, Ill. Aug. 1949". This classic portrait in perfect pose of the SUPER CHIEF, train #18, on a peaceful, no doubt sultry, midwestern Summer afternoon, invites the viewer to remember the smell of creosote on the ties, along with the shimmering heat waves that surely accompanied the brief pause of the Great Train in a scene from a time not really so long ago. (Ed Janosky photo; author's collection.)

Observation end of a "Vista" series car. Pullman-Standard's post-war production of this style of car toward the "cookie cutter" approach. Although the cars did not possess any of the eye-catching interior attributes of "Navajo" or "Puye" they did offer the first class traveler elegant surroundings to "lounge" in, in a tailored, if " vanilla" sort of way. Note the Venetian blinds that have been raised to reflect the actual proportions of the windows in the lounge. (The Kansas State Historical Society).

Shown here is the forward end of a "Vista" observation lounge. Basically the series cars were an updated version of the 1938 four drawing room, one double bedroom cars, which contained no buffet and didn't offer bar service. Apparently meeting Santa Fe's needs for this type of accommodation, their interior configuration was never duplicated by Pullman-Standard for another railroad. (The Kansas State Historical Society, Topeka, Kansas.)

Left: One of the 1938 Pullman-Standard sleeper observation lounges of *CHIEF* lineage, shown here at LAUPT serving the *SUPER CHIEF*. (Santa Fe Railway photo by R. Collins Bradley; author's collection.)

Above: "Biltabito's" observation lounge wasn't flashy like "Navajo" or "Puye", but had a rock-solid, dependable, art-deco look, showing off its metal trim and glossy woodwork in a way that was reminiscent of a swanky club or hotel lobby of the day. Note the only draperies in the lounge shroud the window in the rear door, under which is printed the car's name. (Pullman-Standard.)

In it's second year of service, "Vista Canyon" is shown in special service in Tulsa, Oklahoma on November 6, 1949. Note the unusual appearance without a drumhead. (Collection of Jay Williams and Big Four Graphices.)

Looking picture-perfect, almost like an ad for an electric (model) train, one of the "Vista" observation cars brings up the rear of what must have been a special movement, at Topeka, Kansas, date unknown. Note the "generic" Sante Fe drumhead. (The Kansas State Historical Society, Topeka, Kansas.)

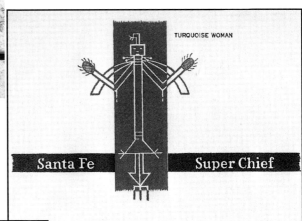

Stationery and envelope used on *SUPER CHIEF*. (Author's collection.)

American Car Foundry's "Vista Club" was the last round-end observation car the Santa Fe ever had built. Compare it's fluting (above the windows) to one of the Pullman-Standard "Vista" cars. (Bob's Photo).

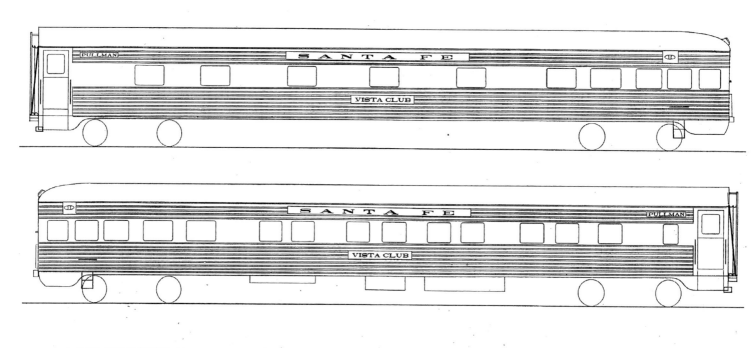

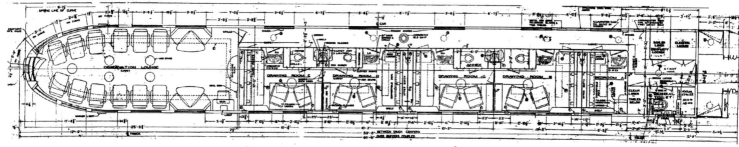

(American Car and Foundry)

A.C.F. "Vista Club" flashes the markers of the *SUPER CHIEF* in the period between the 1951 introduction of the "Pleasure Dome" and the squaring off of it's observation cars in 1956. In the background is Mount Baldy. (Robert O. Hale photo, M.D. McCarter photo collection.)

American Car and Foundry's only entrant in the streamlined observation car roster of the Santa Fe was "Vista Club." This shot, taken April 23, 1966, shows the car in mid-train service at Albuquerque, New Mexico, a little over two years shy of retirement. (Harry Stegmaier.)

The Chief

The first style of observation car the *CHIEF* featured was heavyweight, as illustrated here. It would be followed by observation cars of several others types in the thirty plus years following the train's inauguration in 1926. (The train itself ran for forty-two years.) Note the wooden folding chairs for passengers willing to brave the cinders and wind to view the passing scenery from its open platform, itself a mark of distinction. (The Kansas State Historical Society, Topeka, Kansas.)

The *CHIEF* burnished Santa Fe's rails for 42 years starting in 1926. It served as the railroad's premier all-Pullman train until the inception of the *SUPER CHIEF* in 1936. During its pre-streamlined years, it, too, featured open platform sleeper-observation cars, containing 2 drawing rooms and 3 compartments, first of the "Silver" series with cars such as "Silver Bay", then of the "Crystal" series, e.g. "Crystal Ridge" and "Crystal Bluff". Trains #19 and 20 ultimately became the A.T.&S.F. train that featured the greatest variety of observation car equipment. When it was streamlined in 1938, Pullman-Standard provided "Betatahkin," "Biltabito," "Chaistla," "Chuska," "Coconino," and "Denehotso" using the enduring, unique-to-Santa Fe four drawing room, one double bedroom observation lounge (with no buffet) arrangement that would follow with the construction of "Puye" and later the "Vista" cars. Art-deco in styling, extensive use was made of metal trim, even down to the lampshades in the lounge, which seated seventeen. Though lacking the startling decor of the first two lightweight *SUPER CHIEF* observations, these cars had a solid, dependable, and reliable look to them when viewed now, photographically. A console radio was placed near the writing desk underneath the area usually covered by the photo mural in the *SUPER CHIEF* observation cars, curiously missing in these. The cars are easily differentiated externally from the "Vista"-series by the wide band of flat stainless steel above the exterior windows, (which automatically denotes their pre-War construction) as well as the fact that these earlier cars did not have the light placed at the roof-line above the rear door. (Out of the entire fleet of twenty-five round-end cars, these six cars along with "Puye" were the only ones lacking the latter feature.) Starting in the Fall of 1954 and continuing into the following year, these tail-cars were systematically removed from *CHIEF* service and converted to butt-ended Pullman sleeper-lounges. (Lost, too, in 1954 was the *CHIEF's* all-Pullman status, with the addition of chair cars.) They never returned to their original assignments, but were placed instead in the consists of the last new *CHIEF* to be inaugurated, the *SAN FRANCISCO CHIEF*. R.W. Boyle remembered an interesting "sidelight" to the post-rebuilding use of the line's observation cars. Routine turning on of all lights in the electrical cabinets, such as in Chicago at the beginning of a run, by car attendants or trainmen, would illuminate the markers mid-train. Causing confusion to those inspecting the train passing stations and at other locations ultimately led to their removal. In 1958, these cars were displaced by the "Vista" cars, put into temporary storage (with the exception of "Puye" and "Denehotso" which continued to serve until 1968 as Pullman lounges) until the period of 1960-1962 when the

aluminum, its interior featured one compartment, one drawing room, and three double bedrooms as well as buffet facilities, (where eight patrons could be seated at two tables,) serving the observation lounge, which accommodated 19. Externally, a curious combination of both heavyweight and lightweight construction, it had been built in 1933, (some sources say 1931) was displayed at Chicago's Century of Progress the same year, and certainly was an example of a brief transitional period in passenger car-building. During its career, it served on the *TREASURE ISLAND SPECIAL*, *FLORIDA ARROW*, and *CITY OF SAN FRANCISCO*. Its final years were spent on the Chicago Great Western, going to the scrap line in 1964.

During this remarkable era, starting with a veritable cavalcade of Santa Fe streamliner beginnings in 1938, Budd provided the Santa Fe with a number round-ended cars, all of which were easily identified by the "helmet" of smooth stainless steel that covered the rounded portion of the car's roof (including top-mounted Mars light, and marker lights extending down to the rear window tops) for a short distance forward, which led into the remainder of the roof which was fluted.

Not only the observation ends of the trains were popular places for good Public Relations shots. Here, we see several "Cowgirls" of the era appearing on the front end of the "Mae West," (the alternative nickname steam engine #3460, the "Bluebird" was known by,) arguably the Santa Fe's most famous steam locomotive. (The Kansas State Historical Society, Topeka, Kansas.)

rear observation windows were blanked and the cars converted to coaches. "Denehotso" is currently included in the collection of the Arizona Railway Museum and is undergoing interior restoration. These ex-*CHIEF* cars were numbered in the high 2700s continuing on into the 2800 series of cars at the time of their final rebuilding.

Due initially to "Chaistla's" early substitute service on the *SUPER CHIEF* , the *CHIEF*, at various times from its streamlining to a period following World War II, was short an observation car. Pullman pool car "George M. Pullman," usually filled the void. Constructed solely of

Sante Fe's lone Alco DL 109 cab #50 assaults Edelstein Hill near Chillicothe, Illinois in this July 2, 1942 view of the *CHIEF*. A scant year in service, only eighteen more would follow before it's retirement in 1960. Notice the nose cone that was installed as a war-time security measure to lessen glare from the headlight with the hope of avoiding enemy detection. This unit also performed poorly over the mountains and spent the bulk of it's years on more level midwest trackage. It often served *KANSAS CITYAN/CHICAGOAN*. (Paul Stringham photo, William Raia collection.)

"George M. Pullman" is shown at on the rear of the eastbound *CHIEF*, train #20, in 1947, near Las Vegas, New Mexico. This one-of-a-kind car provided substitute observation car equipment on the train, beginning in 1938, when "Chaistla" spent time serving the *SUPER CHIEF*, prior to the arrival of "Puye." Note the interesting blend of components of both heavy- and light-weight car construction. (Darrell L. Ingersoll, collection of Gordon C. Bassett)

One of the many features of the extensive "Chief" way was the varied scenery offered for the enjoyment of its passengers, simply owing to the enomous geographical area the railroad covered. For the first eight years of its operation, the streamlined CHIEF usually was steam-powered. During that era, it is shown amidst God's handiwork at an often unidentified western location, near an imposing stone cliff. (Santa Fe photo, Harry Stegmaier collection.)

This early 1950s nocturnal view of the CHIEF at San Bernardino highlights one of its sleeper observation lounges that had been in service since 1938. Note the metal-shaded lamp illuminating the lounge. (Robert O. Hale photo; M.D. McCarter photo collections.)

Another perspective of the CHIEF, taken at night in San Bernardino. A nostalgic view that makes the spectator want to take the train, and yet unhappy in the knowledge that trains like this will never again run. (Jay Williams & Big Four Graphics.)

Unexpected in a *CHIEF* consist, "Navajo" is shown on its hind end at San Bernardino, California in 1949. The largest draw-back to this substitute service was the fact that the car's interior configuration bore scant resemblance to the sleeping accommodations of the regularly assigned sleeper observations of either the *CHIEF* or *SUPER CHIEF*. Note the three reminders of a bygone era in railroading in the background. (The Kansas State Historical Society, Topeka, Kansas.)

A 1950's view at Devore, California shows a gleaming *CHIEF*, punctuated by a 1938 Pullman-Standard sleeper-observation lounge. Note the smooth steel roof. Unfortunately, little time remained for the train's consist to end as a classic a 1930's-designed streamliner should....these observation cars were about to vanish forever from trains #19-20. Apparent recent servicing has provided fresh paint on the train's trucks. (Robert O. Hale, photograph, M.D. McCarter photo collection.)

Like stepping back in time..... this photo was captioned by the photographer "Northbound at Joliet, Ill. August 1950." After twelve years in service, the observation lounge of the *CHIEF* at Joliet Union Station reflects the pride the Santa Fe took in maintaining its magnificent fleet. An hour and three minutes and 34.3 miles later, train #20 will break to a smooth stop at Dearborn Station, downtown Chicago, following a trip of 2223.7 miles from Los Angeles Union Passenger Terminal. (Ed Janosky photo; author's collection.)

Train #20, the eastbound *CHIEF* is shown here being serviced at San Bernardino. Unusual in its consist is the presence of "Navajo", long associated with the *SUPER CHIEF*. Taken in 1949, little time remained before "Vista Club" arrived from ACF, in effect keeping the 1937 car largely mothballed until its "official" retirement in 1957. (BNSF Archives.)

El Capitan

Among them were two fifty seat coach observation cars, #3198 and 3199 for the highly popular, all coach *EL CAPITAN*. Following World War II, their passenger capacity was reduced to thirty-six prior to *EL CAPITAN's* service becoming daily in 1948. The New Jersey Department of Transportation acquired the cars in the 1969-1970 period, after they were square-ended in 1961-62.

As we have seen previously, lightweight observation car acquisition on the A.T.& S.F. was a sometimes piecemeal, one-car-at-a-time proposition that tended to produce one-of-a-kind cars. Such was the case with Pullman-Standard-built #3197, (last of the pre-War Pullman-Standard round-end cars built for the Santa Fe; built in 1940) another fifty-seater that ultimately traveled the entire system, many times serving *EL CAPITAN*, sometimes showing up in special service, and in the end somehow dodged squaring-off, scrapping and surviving at least one wreck to become the second of only two of the railroad's round-ends to survive in that configuration.

"Chaistla" poses next to one of the first two *EL CAPITAN* Budd coach-observation cars: either 3198 or 3199. Note differing tailsign applications. (Santa Fe Railway photo, author's collection.)

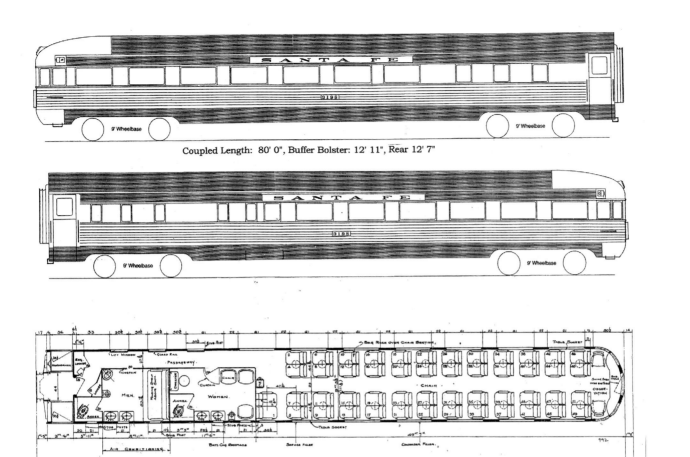

Floor plan of the original *EL CAPITAN* coach observations, cars # 3198- 3199. Note the inward swinging sash (hinged rear-center window) common to all Budd observation cars of the Santa Fe. The two "non-revenue" chairs appear sandwiched in behind the last row of coach seats. (Budd)

Along with the two original Budd cars, it carried a small, glass-shaded "toad-stool"-shaped lamp at its rear window. Like the other pre-War Pullman-Standard-built sleeper observations, this car could always be differentiated from others by the wide strip of stainless steel at its roofline. In this car only, the letterboard was housed on this strip. All Santa Fe Pullman-Standard observations had smooth steel roofs.

In 1947, with daily service in view the following year for *EL CAPITAN*, Pullman-Standard again was called on, this time to supply the final coach observation cars for the company. Cars # 3246, 3247, and 3248 arrived with forty-two coach seats. Missing the tell-tale wide strip above the windows, these cars were fluted to the roof-line. By the time they arrived, the little lamp at car's end had been replaced by a small light placed on either side of the under-window ledge, that could be made use of during night-time hours, no doubt utilizing postcards or the train's stationery by many passengers over the years. Lack of the rear door mandated some form of emergency escape capability, which was again provided by hinging the rear window. This was also the case in the rear of all Budd-built observation cars of the line.

The time of transitioning in the mid-fifties for the round-end cars, also effected the road's premiere coach train. With the introduction of the stunning, all High-

Level *EL CAPITAN* in 1956, its six coach observations became redundant, and available for other assignments. Though the company was still basically displeased with the extra time and effort involved in dealing with the cars, they were, however, placed on the back of the *CHIEF*, which necessitated the train's sleepers running at the head-end. (Because of the re- equipping of trains #21 and 22, it also became possible for the *CHIEF* to be assigned full domes, which they carried until their discontinuance in 1968, at which time low level lounges were replaced with full domes on the *TEXAS CHIEF*.) Still an enthusiastic pro-passenger railroad, many-times coach-starved, the Santa Fe could free-up standard streamlined coaches for other assignments by utilizing these cars in this way, in a service which lasted sporadically until 1959. From that time until their use was discontinued in the early 1960's, the *CHIEF's* famous red backgrounded drumheads, (unchanged since the train commenced service) with the Indian chief's profile and railroad logo, simply rode the rear car, whether coach or sleeper.

Like the *SUPER CHIEF*, *EL CAPITAN*, during its long and proud career showed off two drumhead designs: initially (and years later reverted to) was red, yellow, black and white featuring both vertical and horizontal lettering, in both cursive and block style, including the

Santa Fe logo. The second style, with the implementation of the all High-Level consists in 1956 was a "conquistador" style showing a man's head in helmeted profile against a background of tan, with the train's name printed below in calligraphy-styled letters. In the latter years of operation, the combined train used a simplified drumhead design of a yellow-background lettered with both train names. Budd-produced parlor-observation cars # 3240, 3241, 3242, 3243, and 3244 also arrived in early 1938.

. For decades, the Santa Fe arranged for authentic Indian guides to ride the *SUPER CHIEF* and *EL CAPITAN* within the State of New Mexico to give a running commentary to passengers on the passing landscape, also imparting their knowledge of the local folklore. (So popular was the practice, that it lasted into the Amtrak era.) This photo shows a young passenger enjoying just that in one of *EL CAPITAN's* coach observation cars. Note one of the "non-revenue" seats, barely visible just behind the coach seat. (The Kansas State Historical Society, Topeka, Kansas.)

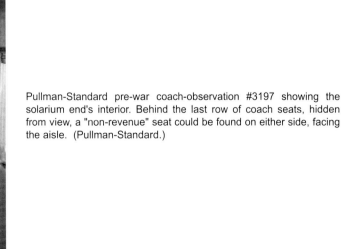

Pullman-Standard pre-war coach-observation #3197 showing the solarium end's interior. Behind the last row of coach seats, hidden from view, a "non-revenue" seat could be found on either side, facing the aisle. (Pullman-Standard.)

"Boat-tail" vs "Teardrop": An interesting study in post-war Pullman- Standard observation car construction, as Los Angeles Union Passenger Terminal hosts departures of two famous streamliners heading for Chicago: Santa Fe train #22 *EL CAPITAN* and Southern Pacific/Rock Island train #4, the *GOLDEN STATE*. On the left, either #3246, 3247, or 3248 coach observation and either #478 "Golden Vista" or #479 "Golden Divan," sleeper-lounge observation on the right illustrates plainly the difference in shape of the solarium ends, even if both were constructed by the same builder. The photo was taken March 28, 1953. (R.S. Plummer, collection of Gordon C. Bassett.)

The combined *SUPER CHIEF/EL CAPITAN* used a combined drumhead, simpler in design from previous years. (Stan Repp photo, author's collection.)

Chicagoan
Kansas Cityan
Tulsan

Cars #3241 and 3242, equipped with thirty-four parlor chairs and eight differently styled chairs in the observation lounge, were part of two identical trainsets servicing trains #11 and 12, the *KANSAS CITYAN* and *CHICAGOAN* on the original Chicago-Wichita route (later expanded,) on opposite daytime schedules for nineteen years. When the *TULSAN* , trains #211-212 was introduced in 1939, parlor service was expanded using the same two cars that were handed off among the three trains at Kansas City. Ever faithful to detail, Santa Fe provided tailsign (all uniquely originally fashioned in green, white and gold, illustrating the train's name and railroad logo with unique art-deco lettering) storage adjacent to the baggage rack of each parlor car, so that the *TULSAN* departing its namesake city, bearing its own tailsign would have it changed in Kansas City to correctly read *CHICAGOAN*; the same process being repeated in the reverse operation; trading the *KANSAS CITYAN's* insigne (having been installed at Chicago) to again read TULSAN. In this service and on all the chair-observations (of both builders) of the road, only the face of the drumhead needed to be changed as needed with varying train assignments. Since their placement was virtually flush with the sweeping silhouette of the car's rear end, the typical "can" of the drumhead was unnecessary, unlike the fastened-on illuminated medallions used on all but one of the Pullman-Standard sleeper-observations.

When the crushing passenger demands of World War II caused even the most antiquated equipment the railroads could dredge up to be utilized, these parlor observation cars helped take up at least a little of the slack by housing overflow, up-graded coach travelers. When my father was overseas during that era, my mom was working in Kansas City. Coach reservations long gone even by Labor Day, she rode in one of the parlors home to Fort Madison for Thanksgiving. Close monitoring was made of seat assignments, using the small metal numbers attached to each parlor chair.

Although their schedules and routes differed in their years of operation, trains #11 and 12 endured for thirty

The Famous Santa Fe Fleet

★ **SUPER CHIEF**
All Private Room, Chicago-Los Angeles Streamliner

★ **THE CHIEF**
Pullman and Chair Car, Chicago-Los Angeles Streamliner

★ **TEXAS CHIEF**
Pullman and Chair Car, Chicago-Texas Streamliner

★ **SAN FRANCISCO CHIEF**
Pullman and Chair Car, Chicago-San Francisco Streamliner

★ **EL CAPITAN**
All Chair Car, Chicago-Los Angeles Streamliner

★ **THE GRAND CANYON**
Pullman and Chair Car, Chicago-Grand Canyon-Los Angeles Train

★ **KANSAS CITY CHIEF**
Overnight Pullman and Chair Car, Chicago-Kansas City Streamliner

★ **KANSAS CITYAN-CHICAGOAN**
Daytime Streamliner, Chicago-Kansas City-Oklahoma City

★ **TULSAN**
Kansas City-Tulsa Streamliner

★ **GOLDEN GATE**
2 Daily Coordinated Bus-Streamliners, Los Angeles-San Francisco

★ **SAN DIEGAN**
4 Daily Streamliners, Los Angeles-San Diego

Santa Fe used the back of its tickets to demonstrate what a full fleet the "Chief Way" had. With the exception of the *TEXAS CHIEF* and the *KANSAS CITY CHIEF*, all the listed trains had featured observation cars of some description in their regularly assigned consists at an earlier point in their careers, even if the *GRAND CANYON's* was heavyweight with an open observation platform. By the time this ticket was issued at Fort Madison August 6, 1967, the cars, as built, were just memories. (Author's collection.)

years. After the cars' retirement in 1957, they remained idle for two years, at which time they were re-built into standard-end coaches at the Topeka shops. (Interestingly, since the coach- and parlor-observation cars were always destined to be used as coaches only following rebuilding, no effort was made to add fluting to the car ends to dress them up for possible end-of-train service. Consequently they became virtually undetectable as former round-ends, except to the discerning passenger car fan's eye.)

Just prior to their removal from service, the *KANSAS CITYAN* became Second 19, when it lost it's own number from Chicago to Kansas City. For a short time, it still carried the parlor-observation car and, in conjunction with First 19's use of the displaced *EL CAPITAN* coach observations, the CHIEF became the train that won the distinction of having used the most types of tail-end equipment in the railroad's history.

With These Superb New Fliers, Santa Fe Adds

2 More Streamliners

To America's Greatest Fleet of Ultra-Modern Trains

● For years there has been a demand for swifter and more convenient daily rail service between Chicago, Kansas City, Topeka, Wichita and intermediate points . . .

It is Santa Fe's privilege to meet this demand with *The Chicagoan* (No. 12 eastbound) and the *Kansas Cityan* (No. 11 westbound)—two superb new trains streamlined in stainless steel, the last word in modern train design.

Speed

The speed of the schedules given the new trains will be apparent from a glance at the timetable shown in the next column. East or westbound, the time between Chicago and Kansas City, 451 miles, is but 7½ hours; between Kansas City and Wichita, 4 hours; between Chicago and Wichita, 665 miles, only 11¾ hours.

Convenience and Economy

Business men in Chicago, Kansas City, Topeka and Wichita naturally have been quick to grasp the advantages of this new service for trips to or from the many important points along the actual route of the new trains. Its convenience is not confined to this area, however.

The Chicagoan and Kansas Cityan permit the fastest schedules yet available, in both directions, between Kansas City, and many Kansas points, and a vast business territory north and east of Chicago to the Atlantic coast.

To economy in time, The Chicagoan and Kansas Cityan add economy in actual travel dollars. Only low-cost coach fare tickets are required, except in the parlor-observation cars, where first-class tickets are necessary. There is no extra fare.

Smooth Power · Beauty · Comfort

The Chicagoan and Kansas Cityan are twin trains of stainless steel, drawn by 1800 H.P.

SCHEDULES		
Westbound		Eastbound
The Kansas Cityan		The Chicagoan
9:30 AM Lv....Chicago....Ar.		9:30 PM
10:13 AM Lv......Joliet....Ar.		8:36 PM
11:00 AM Lv....Streator....Ar.		7:44 PM
11:35 AM Lv...Chillicothe...Ar.		7:05 PM
12:17 PM Lv...Galesburg...Ar.		6:24 PM
1:10 PM Lv...Ft. Madison...Ar.		5:37 PM
2:40 PM Lv....La Plata....Ar.		4:15 PM
5:00 PM Ar...Kansas City...Lv.		2:00 PM
5:15 PM Lv...Kansas City...Ar.		1:45 PM
5:56 PM Ar....Lawrence....Lv.		1:02 PM
6:25 PM Ar....Topeka....Lv.		12:33 PM
7:29 PM Ar....Emporia....Lv.		11:28 AM
8:38 PM Ar....Newton....Lv.		10:20 AM
9:15 PM Ar....Wichita....Lv.		9:45 AM

(Flag Stop

Diesel-electric locomotives. Each includes a baggage car, 3 ultra-modern 52-seat chair cars, a cocktail lounge combined with a 26-seat chair car, a 48-seat Fred Harvey diner, and a 34-seat parlor-observation car.

Throughout the trains, air-conditioned from end to end, beauty, comfort and personal convenience have been stressed in interior decorations, fine lighting, sponge-rubber cushioning of all seats; deep carpeting, broad windows, and spacious toilet-lounge rooms.

In this Santa Fe year, we take keen pleasure in presenting to you The Chicagoan and The Kansas Cityan, and the new and improved service they have made possible.

Passenger Traffic Manager, Santa Fe System Lines.

Chicago, May 14, 1938.

Another *Santa Fe* *New* Streamlined Service....

1938 is a Santa Fe Year

Below: Trains #11 and #12 endured for thirty years and were consistently popular trains. For nineteen of those years (after the *GOLDEN GATE* and *SAN DIEGAN* observation cars were quickly converted from parlors into coaches) they featured the only streamlined parlor-observation cars on the system. The 1938 brochure continued to understandably tout the Budd-built train's facilities in pictures. The center-positioned round-framed photo shows one of the parlor-observation cars in a unique view from the back of the car. Wide-aisled, spacious comfort is the unspoken message relayed here. Note the dated console radio near the bulkhead at the front of the parlor lounge. (Robert Haben collection.)

for Fastest, Finest, Most Convenient and Economical Daily Service Ever Offered
Between **Chicago — Kansas City — Topeka — Wichita**

Santa Fe **Chicagoan · Kansas Cityan**

(Robert Haben collection.)

Above and Right: Seen here in 1938 views, are the two cars that very early in their careers became the only streamlined parlor observation cars on the line. The two Budd-built cars, #3241 and 3242, served the *KANSAS CITYAN, CHICAGOAN*, and *TULSAN*, trains #11, 12, 211, and 212 exclusively in their nineteen year (round end) career, ending in 1957. In a unique three train hand-off rotation that took place daily in Kansas City, Tulsa-Kansas City-Chicago parlor service was maintained that began soon after all three trains commenced service in 1938 and '39. (The Kansas State Historical Society, Topeka, Kansas.)

Floor plan of the *KANSAS CITYAN/CHICAGOAN* parlor observation cars, #3241 and 3242. Note end table (or below-window ledge) common to all Budd observation cars of the Santa Fe as well as the differing style of chairs in the parlor section from the eight in the rear solarium. Photos of the cars show a spaciousness between the rows of parlor chairs not perceived in this drawing. (Budd)

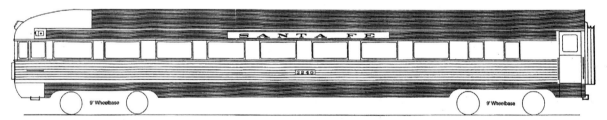

Coupled Length: 80' 0", Buffer Bolster: 12' 11", Rear 12' 7"

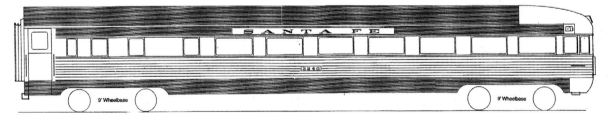

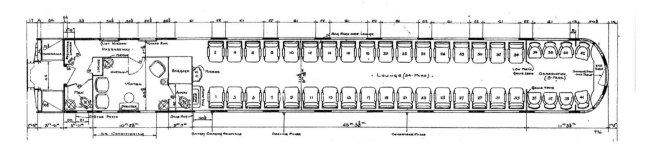

Close-up of the interior of the *CHICAGOAN/KANSAS CITYAN/TULSAN* parlor observation's rotunda. Note the different styling of eight chairs placed in the solarium versus the typical lounge style chair used in the parlor section as well as the antimacassars on each chair display both *KANSAS CITYAN* and *CHICAGOAN* names. (The Kansas State Historical Society, Topeka, Kansas.)

Pocket-sized timetable of the *CHICAGOAN* and *KANSAS CITYAN* from 1966. Their parlor observation cars gone nine years, by this time, the trains themselves would follow two years later. (Author's collection.)

Passenger Schedules

the **Chicagoan**
and
Kansas Cityan

Daily Streamliners between

Chicago-Kansas City-Oklahoma and Texas

Issued September 15, 1966

Santa Fe

San Diegan/Golden Gate

One of the 1938 Budd-built coach observations is seen boarding passengers at San Diego in 1953. Fifteen years of continual service have begun to take their toll, yet its classy design and appearance still makes you want to join the others getting aboard. (Robert O. Hale photo; M.D. McCarter collections.)

Cars #3240, 3243, and 3244 lasted in parlor service in California a disappointing three months. Apparently, dismal parlor business called for the cars to be converted into 58 seat coach observations in short order for their operation on trains # 70-83 the *SAN DIEGAN* operating Los Angeles-San Diego and #60-63 *GOLDEN GATE* on the Oakland (Richmond)-Bakersfield run. As in all the road's coach-observations, each car held two "non-revenue" inward-facing chairs at the rear of the car. Common to all, also, was an unusual interior conclusion to a coach; abrupt car-ending in solarium style, yet not with the usual or expected lounge area. Just prior to war-time, in 1941, Budd supplied its last observation car to Santa Fe in another 58 seater, #3245, assigned to additional *SAN DIEGAN* and *GOLDEN GATE* service. Stated plans of adding a rear-end door to this car were never realized. Steadfastly remaining in California service, these cars lasted until 1956 on the *SAN DIEGAN,* when already-declining passenger revenue halted the turning of the trains at the San Diego terminal, in a bid for lessened servicing and terminal costs. The

GOLDEN GATE used them for an additional two years. Although the coach observations normally held down specific assignments, it should be noted that over the years, they were liable to show up at any number of locations across the system. This happened with greater frequency in the later years of their operation when trains they had served, in some cases for decades, no longer required their use. Conversion into standard lightweight coaches, with the elimination of the round-end came in the late 1950's, extending into the early 1960's. Again, the New Jersey Department of Transportation and Amtrak purchased the cars, as had happened with Pullman-Standard Post War observations #3246, 3247, and 3248, at least one of the last three passing into private ownership following it's Amtrak career.

The two California streamliners used a similar form of drumhead....dark blue background with the train's name and Santa Fe logo were used for the greatest span of years. However, the *GOLDEN GATE* design was originally styled at the top with a sunburst design.

Left: Soon after the *GOLDEN GATE* service was initiated, parlor chairs gave way to coach seating in the Budd-built observation cars the train featured. Shown here is Mr. James Duffy inspecting the first style of drumhead used on trains #60-63, with the sunburst at the top. A second design followed simply stating the train's name and displaying the Santa Fe emblem. Note its flush-mounting typical of all Budd-built observation cars of the Santa Fe, whether coach- or parlor, or sleeper-observation. (The Kansas State Historical Society, Topeka, Kansas.)

Below: Floor plan of the single-produced coach observation #3245. Delivered not many months prior to the World War II hostilities commenced, it was Budd's final observation car built for the system. (Budd)

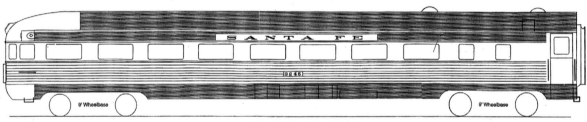

Coupled Length: 79' 3"

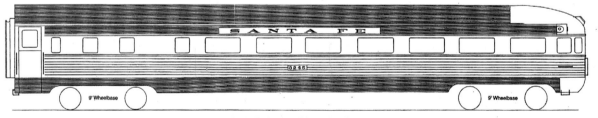

3245 built for San Diegan service.

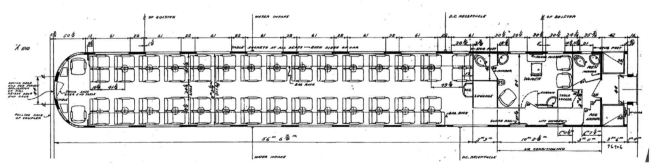

Santa Fe air-conditioned buses meets the brand-new *GOLDEN GATE* in Bakersfield, California, in 1938. The E unit heading up the new train, like many other vintage passenger diesels of the Santa Fe, survived only into the early '50's, as built. (The Kansas State Historical Society, Topeka, Kansas.)

From high atop the Los Angeles post office, the *SAN DIEGAN* is seen threading its way out of LAUPT, its Budd coach observation coupled directly to Santa Fe's lone "pendelum" coach, #1100. Constructed in 1941 by the Pacific Railway Equipment Co., the car's service life of twenty years was spent on the route of the *SAN DIEGAN*. The Burlington and Great Northern owned the other two such cars. (Robert O. Hale photo, M.D. McCarter photo collections.)

Roaring through a gash in the ocean front, the San Diegan's Budd coach observation-equipped *SAN DIEGAN* is shown near Delmar, California in the early to mid-1950s. Note the fluting that extends over the entire roof-top. (Robert O. Hale photo, M.D. McCarter photo collections.)

San Francisco Chief

The final *Chief* to be introduced was the *SAN FRANCISCO CHIEF*, in 1954. With the exception of the Budd-built big domes, which were assigned new to the train, its consist was made up of equipment basically inherited from other trains. Early in its career, a big boost came its way in the form of the displaced sleeper-lounge observation cars of *CHIEF*, which had recently been squared-off. Like the previous two *Chiefs* that had been inaugurated, the *TEXAS CHIEF* and the *KANSAS CITY CHIEF* in 1948 and 1950, respectively, it was a train without an observation car, yet it did feature one in a sense with the introduction of the above-mentioned cars, always placed mid-train. Even though they did not serve in the customary place in the consist, nor were they ever listed as observation cars in the timetable, the Pullman lounges whether from displaced *CHIEF* or, after 1958, *SUPER CHIEF*, (ex-)observation cars remained in the consists for thirteen years, until retired in 1968. For the last seven years of their service, the drawing rooms were sold as compartments. Disposition of the cars is noted in the sections dealing with the *SUPER CHIEF* or *CHIEF*.

Issued April 28, 1963

Welcome
aboard the
San Francisco Chief

We are happy you have selected Santa Fe for your trip. We will do our best to make your journey an enjoyable travel experience.

We hope you have a few minutes to read this folder, study the schedule and get acquainted with these features the San Francisco Chief offers for your enjoyment.

PLEASE LET CONDUCTOR POUCH YOUR TICKET—When the conductor makes his call after you board train he will collect your ticket if you are going beyond his run and give you a receipt from the envelope pouch in which he places your ticket. Tickets are picked up to avoid bothering you each time there is a change of crews. If part of your ticket must be returned, it will be given to you before reaching destination.

BIG DOME LOUNGE CAR is at the center of the train, a friendly meeting place for all passengers.

On the upper level of this car, seats are arranged to give an excellent view of the passing scenery. The lower level has a lounge section for refreshment service until midnight.

A special lounge assigned to Pullman passengers is in the car back of the diner.

Current magazines and newspapers are in the Pullman lounge and Big Dome lounge car.

DINING CAR is located at the center of the train serving Fred Harvey meals at popular prices.

Breakfast service starts at an early hour; Lunch 12 Noon; Dinner 5:30 P.M.

THE COURIER-NURSE. She is a registered nurse and is ready to assist mothers traveling with children and other passengers requiring her assistance.

NEWS AGENT is located in one of the chair cars. He frequently passes through chair cars selling magazines, candy, cigarettes, and novelties.

PILLOWS are available from the news agent. He will be through the chair cars to offer you a pillow, which can be rented for 50¢ for your trip.

RADIOS. Passengers using portable radios will find best reception by placing radio near the window. Please keep the volume low during the day to avoid disturbing neighboring passengers and please do not play the radio during the late hours.

Above: SAN FRANCISCO CHIEF brochure/timetable dated April 23, 1963 making mention of the "Pullman lounge." The cars would last five more years in service, before being retired. (Author's collection.)

Left: This May 27, 1954 view of an abbreviated *SAN FRANCISCO CHIEF*, shows citizens of Wichita, Kansas inspecting the last of the *Chiefs* to enter service. The Big Dome was a part of the train's consist from the very beginning, but its placement on the rear-end of the train, (complete with drumhead,) when in regular service almost assuredly never happened. (The Kansas State Historical Society, Topeka, Kansas.)

Train #2, the eastbound *SAN FRANCISCO CHIEF*, with F unit #312 in charge, glides onto the approach of the bridge crossing the Mississippi River the railroad has owned and operated in Fort Madison, Iowa since it opened in 1927. For decades the bridge was known to possess the world's longest swing span. (Automotive toll-paying traffic uses the upper level.) My Mother was on the first train that crossed the bridge when it opened, and my Father left for and returned from World War II on trains crossing it. My Great Uncle made innumerable trips across it's spans during his Santa Fe career, and I was fortunate to make quite a few with him. (The Kansas State Historical Society, Topeka, Kansas.)

When the A.T. & S.F acquired new high level equipment in 1964, the *SAN FRANCISCO CHIEF* began to include some high level chair cars in its consists, in addition to *EL CAPITAN*. Unusual drumhead placement is shown here at the upper level rather than the lower, where it was usually placed on one of the "step- down" coaches on *EL CAPITAN*. Coaches usually ran at the front of the consist, immediately ahead of the full dome on trains #1 and 2. (The Kansas State Historical Society, Topeka, Kansas.)

Page from R.W. Boyle's "Conductor's Trip Record" showing "Vista Valley" operating as car #29 on train #2, the eastbound *SAN FRANCISCO CHIEF*, September 5, 1967. Note the 216 minute running time, covering 233 miles. (Author's collection.)

R.W. Boyle's Conductor's Trip Record of August 26, 1967 shows "Puye" still in service. Retirement for the car followed in less than a year, after thirty years of continuous service on the *SUPER CHIEF*, *CHIEF*, and *SAN FRANCISCO CHIEF*. Also, soon to be abolished, would be the job of the Pullman Conductor that stilled manned #2 that day. (Author's collection.)

Latter Years Service

Budd-built coach observation #3245, formerly used in *SAN DIEGAN* and *GOLDEN GATE* service, is seen on the former *CAVERN*, behind one of two warbonnetted doodlebugs. Even after this car had been re-built into a standard end coach, pre-war Pullman-Standard coach observation #3197 soldiered on in the same assignment, until 1967, achieving the distinction of being the last AT&SF round-end in service, along with its routine run in tandem with the last two operating doodlebugs on the system. (Mike Gruber collection.)

Following the use of the surplus *EL CAPITAN* coach observations in regular *CHIEF* service, they again became extra equipment that was then conveniently put to use on shorter, sometimes secondary runs, liberating lightweight coaches for transcontinental or at least long distance service, at a time when the company was striving to end heavyweight equipment use, totally. Some of these varying assignments were on the *TULSAN* and *OIL FLYER* (sometimes operating backwards to eliminate switching costs at Kansas City Union Station,) *EL PASOAN*, *TEXAS CHIEF* and it's connection running between Galveston and Houston, Phoenix-Ash Fork, and on the *CHICAGOAN*.

No doubt Santa Fe passenger train enthusiasts will remember certainly the longest running (1956-1967) and oddest service of these cars in the latter years on the train formerly known as the *CAVERN*, known simply in later years by the Santa Fe as Pecos Valley daily streamliner. Paired with the last of the operating doodlebugs dressed up in "Warbonnet" livery, either M.160 and M.190, cars #3245 and 3246 were known to provide occasional service in the earlier years, but best known was the last survivor, the ubiquitous #3197, that prevailed to the very end. Today it and M.160 can still be seen at the "Age of Steam" Museum in Dallas, Texas, keeping silent company with decades of railroad history.

Finally, the last trains displaying drumheads were the *SUPER CHIEF*, *EL CAPITAN*, or their combined train.

Majors factors considered prior to their discontinued used in 1968 were the dual continuing threats of vandalism and theft. Even though a number of trains never used them, (in large measure because of the switching of cars into or out of consists) discerning railfans traveling west from Chicago's Dearborn Station were treated to a glimpse of what the train's missing tailsign would look like by the station's unique custom of adorning bumper posts of departing trains with slightly enlarged drumhead replicas from the 1950s until it closed in 1971. Small drumhead reproductions were also offered for a time as luggage stickers by the A.T. & S. F. Public Relations Department.

Post-war Pullman-Standard ex-EL CAPITAN coach observation #3246 is seen at Artesia, New Mexico February 8, 1960, on the former CAVERN run. Precious little time remains before the Topeka shops will relieve the car of its round end, leaving it an ordinary coach. Note lack of drumhead, compensated for by the rear warning light being built-in, as well as square-window application in marked contrast to the wide windows of #3197. (M. D. McCarter.)

Business Cars

Santa Fe maintained a fairly large fleet of business cars, four of which were lightweight. During the late 1980's and early 1990's, all four were rebuilt. (Several heavyweight business cars were modernized or "stream-styled" over the years, some having received shadow-lining. Division superintendents were at one time provided with a shortened version of a typical heavy-weight brass-railed, open platform office car, many of which lasted into the 1960's.)

Pullman-Standard constructed "Santa Fe" a fluted stainless steel car in 1949. Easily recognized by its pair of extra tall windows on either side enclosing the observation lounge, as well as one on either side of the door to the rear platform, it was designated as the company's president's car. In addition to the observation room, it contained a kitchen, dining room, and four bedrooms, plus sleeping quarters for an attendant. The dining room was equipped with period popularities such as indirect over-head lighting and blonde hardwood furnishings. It's predominant wall held a built-in southwest-style medallion, very similar to the famous one enshrined in the wall of the "Turquoise Room" in the "Pleasure Dome" car of the 1951 SUPER CHIEF. In 1957 the car's name was changed to "Atchison".

At that time, Budd constructed two identical lightweight business cars, with six-wheel trucks called "Topeka" and "Santa Fe", the latter taking over responsibilities for carrying the road's chief executive. They each contained an observation room or lounge at the rear, just inside from the open platform, seating nine people. Continuing forward, four bedrooms, (two with showers,) and a dining room seating eight, were provided along with a kitchen and crew's quarters. The Topeka shops constructed a stainless steel "shroud" for the cars designed to enclose the otherwise open platform that could be attached in times of inclement weather.

In the early 1960's, the fleet was joined by one last lightweight car in the form of ex-U.S. Steel's "Laurel Ridge," originally renamed "Mountainair" by Santa Fe, at the time of it's acquisition. In 1990, it was again renamed "John S. Reed" in honor of the company's president at the time of Amtrak's takeover of passenger operations in 1971. Like "Atchison" the car was a 1949 product of Pullman-Standard. Aside from the fact that the car has no rear platform, the cars are almost identical in interior configuration. The absence of a rear platform makes the car look much like a butt-ended observation lounge. Typical folding streamlined steps that unusually open directly into the rear observation room, make the car an oddity to passenger equipment enthusiasts.

Over the years, not only railroad officialdom, but politicians and show business personalities, as well as special groups have used the facilities of both the streamlined and heavyweight business cars in ways that built valuable goodwill between the company and the public.

One example would be that of President and Mrs. Dwight Eisenhower, during their annual sojourn, to "winter" in California. Ordinarily requesting "Santa Fe", the car would be forwarded to Harrisburg, Pennsylvania over Pennsy trackage from Chicago, where they would board it for the journey west. When Spring rolled around again, they would reverse the process to return home. Mrs. Eisenhower also used the car at the time of her husband's death in1969, journeying to Abilene, Kansas for his entombment.

Santa Fe's business cars served a lot of purposes ....not the least of which was the goodwill built over the years when folks other than railway officials were allowed to use the fleet, and it never hurt when those folks were famous. Here we see Lucille Ball and Desi Arnaz promoting their 1956 feature film "Forever Darling". TV's most popular couple of that era are pictured on the rear platform of Pullman-Standard-built "Santa Fe." Within a year's time, the car's name was changed to "Atchison." (The Kansas State Historical Society, Topeka, Kansas.)

Either business car "Santa Fe" or "Topeka" is shown here in special service for the Air Force Academy. (The Kansas State Historical Society, Topeka, Kansas.)

Floor plan of the Budd-built identical business cars "Santa Fe" and "Topeka." Both cars had six-wheel trucks.(Budd)

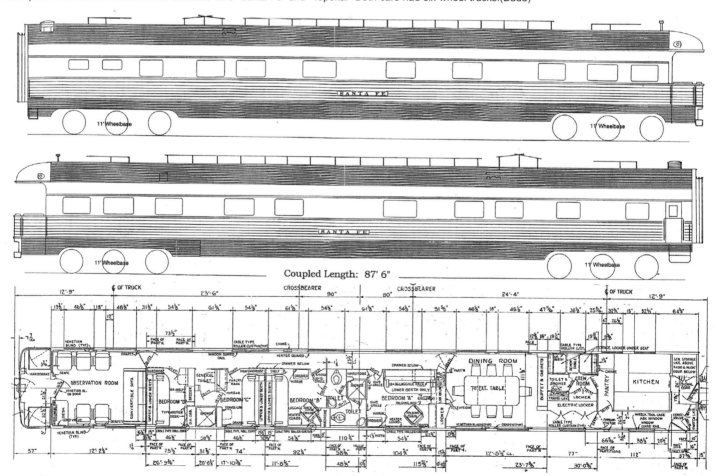

Compare the first streamlined "Santa Fe," built by Pullman-Standard in 1949 to the second built by Budd in 1957.... Both cars, as well as "Topeka", possessed a vastly updated version of the old "brass railed" observation platform....all three were finished off with fluting enclosing the rear platform. All three cars were striking in appearance at anytime, but illuminated at night, with the twin red and clear bulbs on the back of the observation platform operational, one oscillating, they were breathtaking. (P- S)

Pullman-Standard built "Santa Fe" in 1949. Shown here is its dining room, furnished in blonde wood. *SUPER CHIEF* buffs will find the medallion wall-mounted display curiously familiar. (P-S)

1949 "Santa Fe's" observation room featured 2 extra tall windows on either side plus the two flanking the door off the open platform. Notice the stylish indirect "trough" lighting, popular during that era, which provided decidely less harsh illumination than typical overhead fixtures. When my Great Uncle took me through the car in 1966, (nine years after it had been renamed "Atchison,") a color television had been installed, which still wasn't commonplace at the time. (P-S)

President Eisenhower's funeral train, pictured here at Mitchell, Indiana, April 1, 1969, included as it's last car "Santa Fe", (a favorite of the former first couple's) for Mrs. Eisenhower's private use enroute to the former President's entombment in Abilene, Kansas. (Gary Dolzall photo, author's collection.)

While the crew discussed the night's operation of #17, an official already is managing paperwork in the lounge of "Atchison" under the trainshed at Dearborn Station June 23, 1968. Equipped with a large plate glass window, the upstairs waiting room afforded many a railfan panoramic views of train time action. (Richmond S. Bates photo.)

One of the updated "stream-styled" business cars was used in 1958 when the Iowa State University Marching Band and Iowa Highlanders sponsored a special that journeyed to the Tournament of Roses in Pasadena, California. Seen westbound at Fort Madison, the car is sporting two drumheads. 1.7 miles west is Shopton, Iowa, where the train was serviced and engine crews changed. (Conductors and Flagmen changed at Fort Madison.) This arrangement persisted until November 24, 1968 when the "uptown" station closed and all operations were handled at one stop....Fort Madison, the term Shopton no longer officially used. (The Kansas State Historical Society, Topeka, Kansas.)

Modernized business car #31 is seen here March 4, 1967 on Dearborn Station's Annex trackage east of the trainshed. Note the venerable station's clocktower, that still stands at the foot of Dearborn Street in downtown Chicago. (Richmond S. Bates photo.)

Business car #34 can be seen two tracks over from "Atchison" on Track 7, June 23, 1968. Chicago's Dearborn Station. (Richmond S. Bates photo.)

Amtrak

"Wingate Brook" looked a little out of place to the practiced railfan's eyes in Amtrak service, but at least observation cars were again being used, even if sparingly, and for an all too brief time. Here it is shown bringing up the rear of Amtrak's *TEXAS CHIEF* near Galesburg. (Alan Bradley photo.)

In the early years of Amtrak service, streamlined observation cars again rode Santa Fe rails, even if their roots belonged to other railroads.

Amtrak's *TEXAS CHIEF*, later renamed the *LONE STAR*, operated ex-New York Central "Wingate Brook", the tall-windowed 1949 Budd-constructed five bedroom observation lounge (originally built for the "*SOUTHWESTERN LIMITED*") in its consist. It's greatest claim to fame undoubtedly was that, in its capacity as relief car for the "Creek" observation cars of the *TWENTIETH CENTURY LIMITED*, it did in fact operate on the last westbound *CENTURY*, due to the last minute unavailability of "Sandy Creek".

Alternately serving in the same observation position on the train were ex-*CALIFORNIA ZEPHYR* sleeper dome observation cars that featured three bedrooms and a drawing room complete with shower, with an observation lounge seating eighteen including the desk chair. Twenty-four First Class passengers could ride in the dome under which was situated a cocktail lounge. I remember riding one of the CZ cars in this service, with R.W. Boyle, when he was working as a flagman on #15, over thirty years ago, and being surprised that attendants working those cars, (which I had always considered the pinnacle of equipment the Burlington Route offered)

were not overly enthusiastic when they drew them to work, as they considered some of them (using their terminology) "junkers"...complaining that their domes leaked rain among other complaints and that some had apparently been allowed to deteriorate to an unacceptable level. Unfortunately but few passengers realized the railroad history that these cars had played a significant role in, and unless committed railfans, even fewer cared.

In the preceding overview of Santa Fe's signature cars one realizes that they played a limited, yet significant role in the "Golden Years" of passenger trains on the railroad that personified the very epitome of passenger service ever offered. In so doing, these remarkable cars, in many cases now nearly a half century past the rebuilding that partially robbed them of their original individuality, still retain their unique place in streamliner history, brief as it was. It is the author's hope that their story, along with descriptions of the colorful drumheads that accompanied them will not be lost to future generations, and that, along with a few examples of unique motive power used by the Santa Fe during the years the cars operated readers will enjoy reading this book as much as I have in its preparation.

Colors of the Santa Fe

The author and his eldest son, Jonathan J. Boyle, Jr. enjoy "Navajo's" lounge during the Summer of 1985. (Author's collection.)

Still looking sharp after thirty years, "Navajo," the first streamlined observation car constructed for the *SUPER CHIEF* displays the drumhead of owner National Railway Historical Society's Intermountain Chapter. Santa Fe donated the pioneering car, pictured here at Denver, to the society in 1966. (Alan Bradley photo.)

"Navajo's" solarium's interior in later years at Golden is shown in a view taken on a sunny Colorado day. With the signature original upholstery long-gone, "Southwest"-patterned blankets have been lain over the back of the lounge chairs to simulate the earlier years appearance. Notice the framed certificate above the rear window telling of the Santa Fe's donation of the car to the Intermountain Chapter of the National Railway Historical Society in 1966. (Robert Haben Photo.)

The forward end of "Navajo's" lounge displaying the large photo-mural. At right is the writing desk and at left the corridor leading to the sleeper accommodations toward the front of the car. (Robert Haben photo.)

In the year of it's donation by the Sante Fe to National Railway Historical Society, 1966, "Navajo" is depicted on the eastbound *CHIEF*, train #20, at Raton, New Mexico. Note lack of drumhead. (Harry Stegmaier collection.)

Left side of "Navajo's" lounge facing front, the slatted, downward-focused lighting can be seen as well as the "book-case"-style magazine rack. (Robert Haben photo.)

One of the favorite photos from my collection shows pre-war P-S observation sleeper (probably "Puye") running on the *SUPER CHIEF*, no doubt in the period from 1956-1958. Note the old-time markers that have been slipped into small brackets installed when the cars were re-built, needed since the as-built markers had been removed. (Stan Repp photo, author's collection.)

Unfortunately, the end was in sight for the classic car "Puye" when this photo was taken on the scrap-line in Marceline, Missouri during the winter of 1969-70. The original Indian patterned, brightly-colored upholstery had long since been replaced by something more sedate. Though it was built more than thirty years previously for the second streamlined *SUPER CHIEF*, it had also been assigned to the *CHIEF*, intermittently, over the years, and finally served as a mid-train Pullman lounge on the *SAN FRANCISCO CHIEF*. The elegant "swallow-tail" solarium disappeared in 1954. (Alan Bradley photo.)

Contrasting the squared-off, but "prettied up" end of "Puye" next to a standard passenger car. By the time this view was snapped in 1967, at the 18th street coachyard in Chicago, it had been re-configured for thirteen years. Even so, the pains the railroad took to make sure Pullman-Standard's re-building produced a car that appeared properly when assigned to bring up the rear of it's premier train, the *SUPER CHIEF*, are still very evident. (Alan Bradley photo.)

Above and Below: In separate, but dramatic after-dark views, the drumheads of first and second 17s, the *SUPER CHIEF* and *EL CAPITAN* are poignantly illustrated here at Galesburg. The last trains to carry drumheads on the Santa Fe, both tailsigns and the trains that carried them would disappear all too soon, as we remember them. (Alan Bradley photos.)

A Pullman-Standard "Vista" series sleeper-observation seals the end of the ultimate in travel...the *SUPER CHIEF* at Los Angeles Union Passenger Terminal. (Author's collection.)

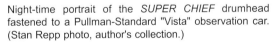

Night-time portrait of the *SUPER CHIEF* drumhead fastened to a Pullman-Standard "Vista" observation car. (Stan Repp photo, author's collection.)

ACF's only contribution to Santa Fe's observation car pool came in the form of "Vista Club." This classic scene, taken September 3, 1955 under Chicago's murky Dearborn Station trainshed illustrates the station's singular practice of adorning its bumper posts with train-identification signs that, at least in Santa Fe's case, matched the train's tailsign in the cases when they were used. Sadly the following year, the "tear-drop" cars were re-built to a butt-ended configuration and two years following that would be removed from the *SUPER CHIEF*, altogether, forever. (John Dziobko photo.)

With drumhead, marker lights, and mars light illuminated, train #18 appears ready to start its eastbound dash to Chicago. Shown at LAUPT, mid-1950's. (Stan Repp photo, author's collection.)

Facing forward from "Vista Canyon's" former solarium, the area now covered by wood paneling originally held a large photo mural. The dining tables were added after the car entered private service. (Arizona Railway Museum collection.)

Little resemblance remains of "Vista Canyon's" observation lounge as built in 1947. The original lounge chairs, extra tall Venetian blinds and draperies are long-gone. Even so, the masterful job Santa Fe required of Pullman at the time of its conversion into squared-ended configuration can still be seen today. (Arizona Railway Museum collection.)

At age 57, little indication remains of the car's swallow-tail origins. Last regular revenue service for the car was on the *SAN FRANCISCO CHIEF* in 1968. (Arizona Railway Museum collection.)

Still used occasionally by its owner in special service, "Vista Canyon," is shown proudly displaying the museum's drumhead. Note small plates that were installed when the original marker lights were removed. Also missing is the light placed above the rear door and the "accordian"-like diaphragm, no doubt worn out many years ago. (Arizona Railway Museum collection.)

The Chief

Above: Color portrait of the *CHIEF's* drumhead, by Stan Repp. The design and coloring of this drumhead remained consistent throughout the train's use of them. (Author's collection.)

Sante Fe's famous #3460, known by railroaders as the "Bluebird" or "Mae West" is shown in Chicago, May 24, 1948. Originally assigned to the 1938 streamlined CHIEF between Chicago and La Junta, Colorado, it soon served a number of other, often secondary, trains. Among them were the ANTELOPE, FAST MAIL, OIL FLYER, and the GRAND CANYON. The massive oil-burning Hudson (which featured seven foot drive wheels) was the only streamlined steam engine the railroad owned and unfortunately suffered a fate similar to a number of early A.T. & S.F. diesels; it was already retired in 1953 at age 15 and on the scrapline at Argentine three years later. (C.H. Kerrigan, Al Chione collection.)

Train #20, the eastbound CHIEF is pictured entering a tunnel as it climbs Cajon Pass, March 20, 1950, showing off one of it's original 1938 Pullman-Standard sleeper-observation lounges. In service for twelve years, only four more remain before it is "bob-tailed." (Chard Walker photo, Robert Schmidt collection.)

After its high-profile days serving on the *CHIEF*, "George M. Pullman" is shown following its purchase by the Chicago Great Western at Oelwein, Iowa in 1950. It went to the scrapline fourteen years later. (Harry Stegmaier collection.)

Interior of the solarium of one of the 1938 *CHIEF* sleeper observation cars as it appeared in an early brochure promoting Santa Fe's burgeoning streamliner service. (Robert Haben collection.)

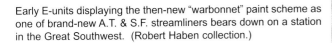

Early E-units displaying the then-new "warbonnet" paint scheme as one of brand-new A.T. & S.F. streamliners bears down on a station in the Great Southwest. (Robert Haben collection.)

Following a "red-cap" down a wooden platform of Dearborn Station getting full benefit of the "Windy City's" icy blasts was made much more palatable when travelers knew their destination would soon be in the sunny Southwest climes of either Arizona or California. One of the 1938 *CHIEF* sleeper-observation lounges is shown proudly displaying the enduring drumhead of train #19. Close inspection of the picture shows the porthole in the door leading forward from of the lounge. (Robert Haben collection.)

Glory years long behind, coach #2812's ancestry is very evident by the fluting that was applied on either side of the diaphragm when it's round end was squared-off in 1954. Originally named "Betatahkin," it functioned sixteen years as one of the "signature" cars of the *CHIEF*. At least on this side of the car, the fluting has been replaced at some point, above the windows. (A give-away to its pre-War vintage, however, can still be seen with the wide strip of stainless steel above the fluting on the re-built car end.) From 1955-1958, it served mid-train on the *SAN FRANCISCO CHIEF* as a First Class lounge. From then until 1960, it remained in storage, when it was re-built a final time as a coach. (Alan Bradley photo.)

After the observation cars were pulled from the CHIEF the drumhead is shown riding the rear Pullman. Not many years passed before the tailsigns themselves were removed from trains #19 and #20. (Stan Repp photo, author's collection.)

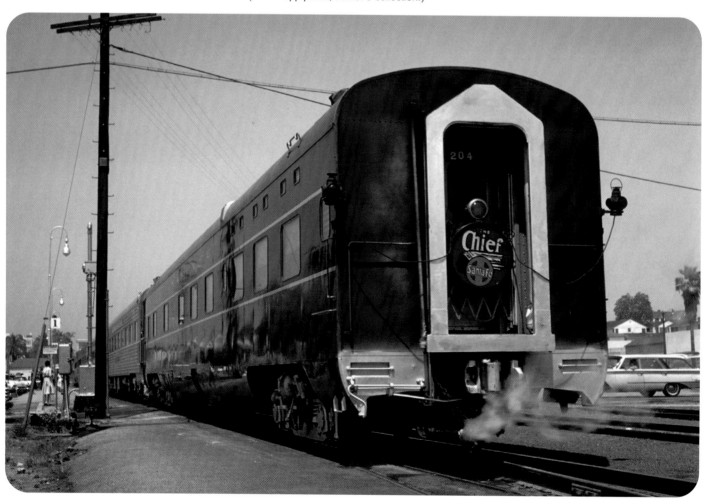

El Capitan

In an early public relations shot, surprisingly in color, a forerunner of the High Level *EL CAPITAN*'s "Courier Nurse" is shown proudly standing next to the famous train's drumhead. (Note car's resemblance to "Navajo.") (Robert Haben collection.)

SANTA FE'S
New Lightweight Streamlined Cars
BUILT BY PULLMAN-STANDARD
THE WORLD'S LARGEST BUILDERS OF RAILROAD AND TRANSIT EQUIPMENT

De Luxe Chair Car—Canyons, Indian pueblos, cattle towns have always made a trip through the Southwest an excursion into romance. Now it becomes more than ever an excursion into luxury, too! For these glistening streamlined beauties covered in stainless steel are dust-proof, air-conditioned and equipped with the latest type reclining chairs.

Constructed in Pullman-Standard's shops for the alert Santa Fe Railroad, this new fleet of lightweight cars is more than a *glittering* example of the progress railroads are making . . . it is also evidence of the influence that you, and travelers like you, have over transportation.

For, in railroading, as in every other field of enterprise, men and institutions may vie for leadership, but only the public has the power to confer it. In making Pullman-Standard-built streamliners the most popular and profitable group of trains on earth, you have done the one thing needed to increase the availability of this modern, safe, luxurious and fast way to travel . . . shown the railroads that you want these trains! Proved to them that wherever they are installed, they will operate at a profit! And, mark this down to the railroads' everlasting credit, confronted with your decision, they have not hesitated, but acted. Acted with such purpose that already over 72%* of the lightweight streamlined units purchased by them have been built by Pullman-Standard.
When this advertisement was written.

In addition to railroad passenger cars, Pullman-Standard designs and manufactures freight, subway, elevated and street cars, trackless trolleys, air-conditioning systems, chilled tread car wheels and a complete line of car repair parts.

PULLMAN-STANDARD CAR MANUFACTURING COMPANY
CHICAGO

The Bar Lounges on these new cars have been called one of the brightest spots in America . . . an honor they fully deserve. For here, encounters among the vacation-bound create a gay, holiday atmosphere.

The Lunch Counter Diner holds one of the pleasantest surprises awaiting you on the new streamlined dining cars built by Pullman-Standard for the Santa Fe . . . Fred Harvey meals, whose economy and excellence are as native to the Southwest as chaps and ten-gallon hats.

"Tops" IN STREAMLINERS ARE BUILT BY Pullman-Standard

Though Pullman-Standard sponsored it, Sante Fe no doubt profited the most from this 1940 ad. Car #3197, with it's "picture" windows, is featured. (Author's collection.)

EL CAPITAN's Pullman-Standard post-war coach observation is shown easing away from a California station stop in the mid '50s. Little time remains before the train will be completely re-equipped with a brand-new consist, something precious few railroads were willing to do by this "late hour" in passenger train history. (Stan Repp photo, author's collection.)

End of an era...In this June 16, 1957 shot taken near Williams, Arizona, the *CHIEF* is shown trailing one of the coach observations that had been made available with the arrival of *EL CAPITAN's* all High Level consists the previous year. This service would prove to be the last regularly assigned use of round-end observation cars on Santa Fe transcontinental trains. (Tom Gildersleeve photo.)

In the early hours of July 6, 1950, eastbound trains #10 and #22, (the *KANSAS CITY CHIEF* and *EL CAPITAN*, respectively), momentarily running side by side, were involved in a high speed derailment at Monica, Illinois, (M.P. 148, between Chillicothe and Galesburg) that resulted in the loss of nine lives. Miracuously, pre-war Pullman-Standard chair observation car #3197 remained upright, still on the rails. (Alan Bradley photo.)

Ultra-modern *EL CAPITAN* beautifully re-equipped with all new High Level equipment in 1956, proudly displays its re-designed drumhead, with a flash of the past shown with the marker lights recalling another era. (Stan Repp photo, author's collection.)

Chicagoan/Kansas Cityan/Tulsan

One of only two streamlined parlor observation cars, (#3241 or 3242) on the system is shown displaying the tailsign of #12, the *CHICAGOAN*, ready to leave Fort Madison, Iowa in 1955. (Less than four hours earlier, it had the TULSAN's drumhead changed for the one seen here.) At left is the venerable brick depot that served the Santa Fe until 1968, soldiering on through two world wars, the Great Depression, the demise of stream and rise of the diesel, and all but three years of the magnificent streamlined *CHIEF's*. (Just to the left of the Santa Fe facility (on parallel tracks) is the Burlington station, which at the time of this photo still hosted the *MARK TWAIN ZEPHYR* and *ZEPHYR-ROCKET* on a daily basis.) When departing the station, the train will begin to bear slightly to the right, then jog slightly left, then right again onto the approach to Santa Fe's 1927-vintage bridge to cross the Mississippi River, one of the few locations where its course runs east and west. (Ed Spitzer, Al Chione collection.)

Parlor Observation car #3242 plied the route of the *CHICAGOAN/KANSAS CITYAN*, (and after a short time the *TULSAN*,) along with it's twin car, #3241 or nineteen years, exclusively. The accompanying photo, of train #11, the *KANSAS CITYAN*, dated September 4, 1956, illustrates one of the many reasons the Santa Fe enjoyed the sterling reputation it did regarding it's passenger trains: following nearly two decades of daily service, equipment maintenance still provides the gleaming "mushroom cap" over the solarium of the car, as well as the fluted sides of the car that shine as the train rolls beneath Mid-western skies. The following year meant the termination of Santa Fe parlor car service, and temporary storage of the two cars until they were square-ended and re-built into coaches. (Harry Stegmaier collection.)

For awhile, the *KANSAS CITYAN*, (after surrendering its independent identity as #11, east of Kansas City) ran as a second section of the westbound *CHIEF*, E units had a long career on the Santa Fe, serving in four different decades, and on the day of this photo, taken at Galesburg, are in charge of second #19. (Alan Bradley photo.)

As the photographer noted, there were "no mountains to cross" which probably accounted for the favorite final Great Plains assignments that were held down by the elegant, but aging E units pictured in these views. Shown here is #12, the *CHICAGOAN* at a momentary stop in Galesburg. (Alan Bradley photos.)

San Diegan/Golden Gate

Fairbanks-Morse Erie-built #90 was at home on the coast line for a number of years, due to early poor performance crossing the mountains. Here it is shown negotiating trackage near LAUPT. At the time of it's retirement in 1963, it had only been in service sixteen years. (Gordon Glattenberg photo.)

This rare color view of the *SAN DIEGAN* showing it's Budd-built coach observation car was taken at Santa Ana, California, July 26, 1951. (Tom Gildersleeve photo.)

Richmond, California is the setting for this September 14, 1957 shot of the *GOLDEN GATE*. The Budd coach observation disappeared from its twenty year assignment on the train the following year. (John Dziobko photo.)

These four photos taken in California in 1956, show a Budd-built coach observation (wielding the blue flag) on the *GOLDEN GATE* in contrast to Pullman-Standard-built coach observation #3197 (running in the consist of an extra movement for the Pacific Railroad Society), along with a close-up of the back of each train. Within the following two years, the observation cars will have been pulled from the *GOLDEN GATE* (where they had run for 20 years), awaiting re-building to standard-end coaches. Illustrated here is the second drumhead designed for the train. (Author's collection.)

San Francisco Chief

This shot, taken at Dearborn Station on April 10, 1971, (just prior to Amtrak's takeover of intercity passenger service and the closing of the station,) shows the drumhead facsimile of the *SAN FRANCISCO CHIEF* mounted on the bumper post of Track 3. In reality, the train hadn't carried a drumhead for years, and by the time this photo was taken, none of the remaining *CHIEFs* did, either. However, the station's custom of identifying departing trains in this way continued until the end. Shown on the ground at right is the sign used for departing train #17, the combined *SUPER CHIEF/EL CAPITAN*. After the *GRAND CANYON* lost its name, a generic Santa Fe herald was used for #23. (Photo by the author.)

Santa Fe's reputation for first class passenger service extended even to the appearance of the engines powering their trains. Here Alco PAs are in charge, eastbound at Galesburg. Built in the period of 1946-1948, the units lasted in Santa Fe service until 1968. (Alan Bradley photo.)

Fifty years after its rebuilding at Pullman's Calumet shops, "Denehotso's" observation end has endured more than three times longer butt-ended, than as-built. In 1978, the car was featured in the movie "Terror Train." (Arizona Railway Museum collection.)

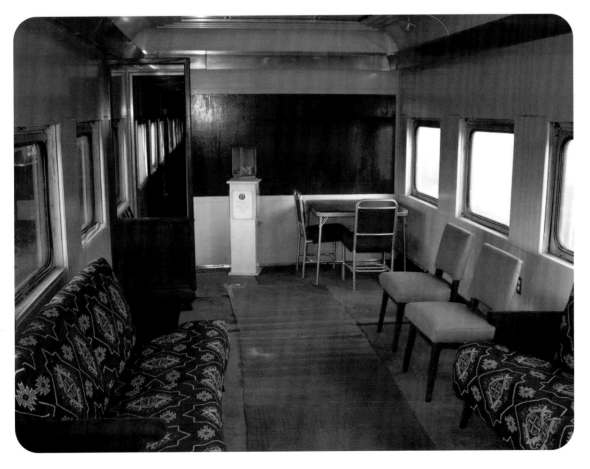

Sixty-six years after it entered service "Denehotso's" observation lounge (facing the front bulkhead) as it appears today. As built, the corridor was protected by a porthole-equipped door. The last car in it's series to survive, the others having been made into coaches and scrapped years ago. (Arizona Railway Museum collection.)

Latter Years

Looking sharp at age 63, chair observation #3197 is shown as it appears today in Dallas, Texas. Note *TEXAS CHIEF* drumhead that has been added in recent years. Just ahead, barely visible is "Doodlebug" M.160, one of the two long-time running mates on the former *CAVERN* run. On rare occasions the flashy pair still make an appearance at a local civic celebration in Texas. (Alan Bradley photo.)

The last survivor, in service at least, and one of the most photographed of the Santa Fe observation cars, #3197 is seen in Dallas, Texas, it's final home. Note the large windows so different from the square-windowed application found in the post-war Pullman-Standard coach-observation cars. May, 1970 (Alan Bradley photo.)

The lone pre-war-constructed Pullman-Standard coach observation #3197, was also winner of the award for last operating round-end observation car on the system. Shown here June 0, 1902, the car had a good five years of service left before it's tenure on the "Pecos Valley Chief" came to a close. (Harry Stegmaier photo.)

October 8, 1966 is the date of this excellent view of the pre-War ex-*CHIEF*, (now butt-ended) observation car "Denehotso". Although the car routinely served Amarillo and other Texas stops for a number of years mid-train on the *SAN FRANCISCO CHIEF*, it's presence at Fort Worth as shown here is somewhat a mystery. Proudly postured in it's old tail-car position, it was probably in service on the *TEXAS CHIEF*; perhaps supplementing sleeper and lounge service, (full domes weren't added until the demise of the *CHIEF* in 1968), maybe providing in a single car for a charter group, or even on a special train. The latter possibility isn't likely...many times groups chartering entire trains displayed a drumhead, such as was the case on many "Shrine Specials." (Harry Stegmaier collection.)

The *CHIEF* drumhead and markers from yesteryear certainly complete a dressed-up portrait of a classic car as it is today. However, it is highly doubtful that the car ever appeared this way in service. Following it's rebuilding, sleeper-lounge observations were never again regularly assigned to the *CHIEF*. The car was also part of the collection at Steamtown, U.S.A. in the years before coming to Arizona. (Arizona Railway Museum Collection.)

Business Cars

Photographer Gordon Glattenberg provided the following caption information: "'Topeka' is at Williams Junction June 12, 1965, on its way to Grand Canyon with [former Santa Fe President] Fred Gurley. The other car is former Soo Line business car 54, then owned by a Southern California railfan group. I was riding it on a San Bernardino-Grand Canyon round trip with about 25 other railfans. As "Topeka" would block our view out the back on the ride up the branch, Mr. Gurley invited us to ride the "Topeka."" (Gordon Glattenberg photo.)

Budd-built "Topeka" is seen here at Colorado Springs, Colorado, September 30, 1979. Equipped with a stainless steel enclosure for the upper, (usually-open) portion of its observation platform built by the Topeka shops for service such as this (when used mid-train) or in the case of inclement weather. (Dr. Robert R. Harmen, author's collection.)

"Mountainair" was an odd car in several ways. In this May 26, 1963 scene at Summit, (on either train #20 or #124,) it bears great resemblance to a butt- ended observation car, certainly not a business car in the ordinary sense. Note lack of rear platform, steps that open directly into the rear lounge, and the slim application of stainless steel fluting on it's flank. (Gordon Glattenberg photo.)

From a head-end perspective, "Mountainair" is shown in the 18th Street coachyard in Chicago. Close inspection shows window placement identical to "Atchison", another 1949 product of Pullman-Standard. Other than "Mountainair's" lack of a rear platform, the car's interiors were also quite similar. (Alan Bradley photo.)

"Wingate Brook" (or one of it's two identical twins, "Singing Brook" or "Sunrise Brook") is shown in service on the COMMODORE VANDERBILT, during it's days on it's native New York Central. (Of the three, only "Wingate Brook" stayed the course to last up until Amtrak. The other two cars were sold to Canadian National and National Railways of Mexico, in 1959 and 1964, respectively.) Other substitute service was provided by the car on the OHIO STATE LIMITED, and the NEW ENGLAND STATES. Who would have thought that the car would ever show up on Santa Fe rails? (Stan Repp photo, author's collection.)

Amtrak

Having fallen victim to Amtrak's garish "updated" redecoration, former New York Central patrons would have found "Wingate Brook" unrecognizable and possibly somewhat alarming in appearance in its Amtrak days on the TEXAS CHIEF, after it's plush, but staid service on the famous TWENTIETH CENTURY. Shown is the forward end of the observation lounge. (Alan Bradley photo.)

Backed in at Chicago Union Station, on #15, Amtrak's TEXAS CHIEF, "Wingate Brook" was again in the passenger-welcoming business. (Alan Bradley photo.)

These two views show a dome sleeper-observation car that had been the "star" of the *CALIFORNIA ZEPHYR* coming into Chicago Union Station's South tracks as it had for nearly a quarter century. In this service, however, it had traveled over one-time rival Santa Fe's tracks, on #16, the Amtrak *TEXAS CHIEF* which would soon become the *LONE STAR*. (Alan Bradley photos.)

This book's author and my Great Uncle, Russell W. Boyle on our last train trip together. We were seated in the rear lounge of an ex-*CALIFORNIA ZEPHYR* dome-sleeper-observation car then assigned to Amtrak train #15, the *TEXAS CHIEF*. (Author's photo.)

Framed in the rear door of one of Amtrak's ex-*CALIFORNIA ZEPHYR* dome- sleeper-observation cars, R.W. Boyle, working as Flagman, stood as train #15, the *TEXAS CHIEF* sped somewhere between Chicago and Fort Madison. He had the uncanny ability to peer out into the darkness anywhere between mileposts 0 and 234 and be able to unerringly give the exact location at any given moment. (Note the typical Budd tunnel-type opening for the inner rear door which could also be found in lightweight observation cars of the Florida East Coast and Seaboard.) The car, though repainted in Amtrak exterior colors, remained unaltered from its *CALIFORNIA ZEPHYR* days in the interior. (Photo by the author.)